T0380317

Inspired Whispers

TAMI S. WYATT

WESTBOW
PRESS®
A DIVISION OF THOMAS NELSON
& ZONDERVAN

WestBow Press books may be ordered through booksellers or by contacting:

WestBow Press
A Division of Thomas Nelson & Zondervan
1663 Liberty Drive
Bloomington, IN 47403
www.westbowpress.com
844-714-3454

Because of the dynamic nature of the Internet, any web addresses or
links contained in this book may have changed since publication and
may no longer be valid. The views expressed in this work are solely those
of the author and do not necessarily reflect the views of the publisher,
and the publisher hereby disclaims any responsibility for them.

Any people depicted in stock imagery provided by Getty Images are
models, and such images are being used for illustrative purposes only.
Certain stock imagery © Getty Images.

ISBN: 979-8-3850-2468-1 (sc)
ISBN: 979-8-3850-2469-8 (e)

Library of Congress Control Number: 2024908723

Print information available on the last page.

WestBow Press rev. date: 5/13/2024

Dedication

To God, my moment-by-moment strength, my refuge in
the storms of life and for the words that You give to me
to inspire others, that they might want to follow You.
To my mom. You have been the one person that I could
go to when I needed spiritual insight. I have watched
you go through many challenges through life and yet
your faith was always at the forefront of the response.
I love you mom. Thank you.

*"After the earthquake came a fire,
but the Lord was not in the fire.
And after the fire came a gentle whisper."
1 Kings 19:12 NIV*

Introduction

Do you ever wake in the middle of the night and lay there with thoughts rolling around in your mind? It happens to me more often than not. I start to pray for each concern and loved one that comes to mind. Then I feel it, not a huge shout or lightbulb, but a whisper. A whisper from my Heavenly Father, giving me a thought, an inspired whisper.

I've been writing poems and short stories for as long as I can remember. I have a whole collection of them in my file. But a few years ago, I started to feel the Lord leading me to write devotional thoughts. As you read through this book, you will see that at first, the stories are not as deep into God's word. Then as you go along, it changes. I have felt a closeness with God that I cannot explain. He gives me a thought and now instead of merely writing out the thought, I'm growing by digging into His Word and getting to truly know Him.

That's what He wants for each of us. To grow.

"Being a Christian, is more than an instantaneous conversion, it's a daily process by where we grow to be more and more like Christ." ~Billy Graham

"But grow in the grace and knowledge of our Lord and Savior, Jesus Christ." 2 Peter 3:18 NIV

Bible Translations Abbreviations

ERV – Easy-to-Read Version

ESV – English Standard Version

EXB – Expanded Bible

LAB – Life Application Bible

MSG – The Message

NASB -New American Standard Bible

NCV – New Century Version

NIRV – New International readers version

NIV – New International Version

NLT – New Living Translation

NOG – Names of God Bible

TLB – The Living Bible

Contents

Dedication..vii
Introduction ix
Bible Translations Abbreviations xi

Guide Me..1
The Bigger Picture.. 2
King Fisher 4
To You 6
Get Serious 7
Standing on the Rock 9
Where Are You?... 10
Keep Hope Alive 14
Just Go 16
Keep... 18
A Good Soul Searching 20
The Good Stuff.. 22
JOY 24
Psalm 23 26
Love His Way 28
Curveball 30
Not Forgotten 33
Control 35
The Simple Answer.. 37
Where Would We Be? 39

Prepared 42

More Time... 44

Joy? 46

Laid Out 49

Sustenance... 51

Reign in My Brain 53

Faith-Full-ness.. 55

Lifted and Able.. 57

"Feed My Sheep"... 60

It Takes a Village 62

Alone 64

Weighted Down 66

"56" 68

Happily, Blessed 71

About the Author 75

Guide Me

The stillness of the morning, how wonderfully peaceful it is.
I can't stop my thoughts from racing around like a whiz.

It's hard to quiet those thoughts when I awake for the day.
So, I take a deep breath in that moment and ask Jesus to stay.

Oh Lord, would you go before me in all that I do?
Help me be a vessel, for Your Glory, help me to pursue.

Help me see and hear what You have prepared for me.
Let me not get stuck in any of the day's negativity.

Thank You for all the times you've proven Your faithfulness.
Even though there are times I go ahead of You and make
a big mess.

Father, I ask that You watch over those that need You.
Help me be a light for them if it's the only thing I can do.

Help it not be about me Lord, but only Your love and
Your way.
Keep me close to You Lord so I can go home with You
someday.

9/25/2020
TSW

The Bigger Picture

"There are many plans in a person's heart, but it is the Lord's purpose that prevails."
Proverbs 19:21 NIV

God sees the bigger picture. He sees. He wrote out each and every minute of your day, today, tomorrow and even yesterday.

Let that sink in. God, the creator of this big vast earth and every living thing on it, cared enough to write every second of your life. The good, the bad and everything in between.

I don't know about you, but that thought is very humbling. Most days I sit, stand and walk in pain. I wonder why things must go the way they do, and at the age of 48, I have a list of limitations. Let's get it straight though, God does not make bad things happen, He allows them. He allows them because He wants us to be on a better path. Just maybe our suffering can be used for His Glory. Just maybe someone else will see Jesus in our perseverance.

Maybe your suffering, your exhaustion, your joblessness, your relationships or maybe your worries and frustrations with family and friends is supposed to put you on a course towards God's better plan. None of us know what our exact purpose is for our lives.

Well, let me tell you. It has ALL been written out by our great big God. It's for us to be diligent in prayer and seeking Him, and if necessary, waiting. It's in the waiting, if we are willing, if we are listening and heeding to His direction for His purpose to lead others to Him.

So, don't think that you must have it all figured out today. All you must do is stay close to the One that already has a plan and breathe in His grace, then exhale and keep on persevering, no matter what your day brings.

7/26/2020
TSW

King Fisher

Every morning for about the last two months when I am on the porch, there is a bird that is constantly calling out and moving from one place to another around the pond. (You see, about two months ago John had minnows put in the pond.) This bird is called a Kingfisher. They feed on small fish in small bodies of water. It makes me wonder why none of his friends or family have come to feed when the eatin is so good! Yet every morning over and over he calls out for someone to hear. To come eat where there is plenty for all.

That's how I imagine it is with God. We call out day after day for our heartaches and our disappointments. Asking Him to fix things. Asking Him to "feed" us with His wisdom so that we can understand life. I don't know about you but I'm REALLY struggling with life right now. I cry when I get off the phone with my mom, whom I haven't visited in three weeks (longest it's ever been, was 10 days!) due to the pandemic shutdown again in nursing homes. Yet, God whispers to me, "Come to Me all who are weary, let Me be your strength and determination to get through every day of the same ole same ole." You see when we cry out to God, He alone provides all we need. He swoops in and fills the gaps!

We may not have the ability to have human in person interactions these days, but we can have Zoom, Facetime, porch visit, make phone calls, write letters, send cards, make baked goods, and do a porch drop or anything else you can think of to keep on trusting God in the uncertainty. When we keep on moving forward in Faith, God can do mighty things!

11-29-20
TSW

To You

As soon as I wake my mind goes to You.

Thank You Lord Jesus for all that You Do

When I'm weary and worn, You stay by my side

With a peace that passes all understanding, in my heart You abide.

And then when I'm shouting with the Joy that you give.

Each and every day walking with You, that's how I want to live.

No matter what the days and weeks might bring.

I look to You Father, for Your mercy.

Of Your grace, I will sing.

10-6-2020
TSW

Get Serious

Are you serious about following God or is it just a "habit" or afterthought? Do you go to sleep praying and wake up praying? Do you spend time with God every day or just when it's convenient?

Matthew 6:28 (NCV) says "Seek first God's kingdom and what God wants. Then all your other needs will be met as well." That rule seems so simple when you read it, but it is a deep, daily, minute-by-minute rule that God wants us to apply to every single area of our lives.

I love how the Message also talks about giving God everything in *Proverbs 3:5-12*, it says, *"Trust God from the bottom of your heart; don't try to figure out everything on your own. Listen for God's voice in everything you do, everywhere you go; he's the one who will keep you on track. Don't assume that you know it all. Run to God! Run from evil! Your body will glow with health, your very bones will vibrate with life! Honor God with everything you own; give him the first and the best. Your barns will burst, your wine vats will brim over. But don't, dear friend, resent God's discipline; don't sulk under his loving correction. It's the child he loves that God corrects; a father's delight is behind all this."*

If you are always struggling with daily responsibilities, health, self-image, co-workers, vehicles, kids...and the list goes on, you must stop focusing on the things of this world that have no heavenly value and seek Him, above all else. You need to get serious about it. You're not going to be satisfied, truly satisfied, until you give God first place.

4-25-21
TSW

Standing on the Rock

Have you ever stood in the sand and watched the water come up around your feet again and again as it crashed on shore? Each time, your feet get deeper and deeper in the sand, sinking...sometimes even getting stuck.

Now imagine standing on a rock on the shore, the water crashing, spraying that beautiful mist all around you. Do your feet sink? No. Because they are standing on a firm surface.

I don't know about you, but I would rather not get stuck in the sands of life. The lies the devil tries to get us to believe. We're not good enough, we're not pretty enough, we need the perfect outfit, or the perfect hair and nails. Oh, and how about.... you've gained a little weight, you've aged?! Folks, those are flat out lies! If you are building on the sand, you could go down real fast! But by spending time in God's truth, every day, you can throw those lies right back to the devil and shout out from the top of the rock "I am who God says I am!"

4-27-21
TSW

Where Are You?

Zephaniah 3:17

ERV
"The Lord your God is with you. He is like a powerful soldier. He will save you. He will show how much he loves you and how happy he is with you. He will laugh and be happy about you."

EXB
"The Lord your God is ·with you [in your midst]; the mighty One will save you. He will ·rejoice over you [take delight in you]. ·You will rest [or He will quiet you; or He won't rebuke you] in his love; he will sing and be joyful about you."

NOG
"Yahweh your Elohim is with you. He is a hero who saves you. He happily rejoices over you, renews you with his love, and celebrates over you with shouts of joy."

NLT
"For the Lord your God is living among you. He is a mighty Savior. He will take delight in you with gladness. With his love, he will calm all your fears. He will rejoice over you with joyful songs."

No matter how you spin it, the Bible is clear... God is with us!

We have all had those days when nothing seems to be going our way and we are ready to scream at the top of our lungs "GOD, WHERE ARE YOU?"

Recently, I had one of these kinds of days. Of all places it was in the local Jo-Ann store while looking for fabric.

You see that morning started off, not on the porch, sipping my coffee and doing my devotions, but with a phone call from a family member that did not make sense. This led my whole morning off in a panic, not a prayer! Off to her house I went. That ending is a whole other story...

Next came the appointment with someone to meet up to buy a dresser that I had listed for sale for my mom who lived 20 minutes in the opposite direction. I waited... messaged them...waited some more. After 30 minutes of waiting, the woman texted and said, "we changed our mind and don't need it after all". Insert fuming emoji face!! WHAT?! I had no choice but to lock up and head to the next item on my list for the day!

My granddaughter's birthday was in 3 weeks and the lap quilt I had made needed 1 more yard of fabric for the backing, so I headed over to the local Jo-Ann store. Walking across the store I knew exactly where to find it. Round about the tower of fabric choices once...twice...

ARE YOU KIDDING ME?! Really Lord! One yard that's all I need! Go figure the flannel was on sale that day and the racks were sparse. I paused, took a breath and prayed. "Lord, why are you not helping me today? Where have you been? I just needed one more yard! Every day I pray and ask you to go before me.... Why not today??" After another breath I walked around the tower and decided maybe they have others up at the cutting table since it is on sale. When I came around the corner the lady was standing there with a cart full of bolts of flannel. I asked her if she minded if I looked through them. I needed coral fabric with white polka dots to finish a quilt I was working on. Just as I am saying that I looked at the fabrics on the tower beside her and right there it was! I literally said, "There it is!" She looked to her side and said, "that was the first one I put back, just now." Insert sobbing emoji face!! I told her right then as I started crying, that I had just prayed in the other aisle for God to show up! I told her she would not believe the day I had had so far!

Now, I'm sure that I am not the only one that has had a day like that. I'm also sure it won't be my last day like that. But it is in those days that God is trying to teach us valuable lessons, or maybe trying to teach others valuable lessons through our response to those days. It is so very important that we don't hide the bad days, trying to handle everything on our own. God gave us each other. God gave us His word, full of promises that tell us, HE IS WITH US! Try to breathe the next time your day starts this way. Instead of grumbling, cry out to God who already knows but wants you to ask for His help in full abandonment. He cares! You can trust His heart!

5-16-21
TSW

Keep Hope Alive

"Abraham believed in the God who brings the dead back to life and who creates new things out of nothing. Even when there was no reason for hope, Abraham kept hoping." – Romans 4:17-18 NLT

Have you ever really listened to the song "Wonderful, Merciful Savior? (LOOK IT UP: BY: SELAH) There is one line in the song that talks about "you offer hope, when our hearts have hopelessly lost their way."

Can you imagine losing ALL hope? I'll have to admit, there have been times when life seems so dismal that I can't breathe. That all the areas of my life crash at once and I'm ready to throw in the towel! Can you relate? God told Abraham that he would have MANY descendants and until he was old...100...He kept hoping! I don't know about you, but the way my body feels daily, I cannot imagine living to be 100 years old and still having that much hope!

It's not about how your body feels, when the world around you is falling apart, or how your job seems overwhelming, or the health and well-being of your loved ones...it's about HOPE! HOPE IN JESUS!

This morning, take a breath before you start your day. If it's already started, find a moment and just breathe in deep...exhale slowly...hum or sing the song... Wonderful, Merciful, Savior. As you do, remember to keep hoping.

7/24/21
TSW

Just Go

If you look up the word isolation you will see lots of things about depression, loneliness, and increased health issues. This past year especially! Isolation leaves us exposed and vulnerable. We are not meant to be alone. Although it may be enjoyable to have peace and quiet and enjoy just doing what WE want to do, it is not what God had in mind for our lives. When we just sit at home, the enemy starts whispering in our ear making us fall back onto our own selfish desires.

Acts 1:8 (NIRV) reads "you will go tell other people about me from one end of the earth to the other." Now, how can we tell others what God has done in our lives or show His love if we sit at home watching TV, scrolling through social media. His Love is about connection!

Sometimes I'm uncomfortable speaking up about what God has done in my life. Maybe because the person(s) I'm visiting just do not understand or believe in God. Maybe it's because they've gone through a really rough time recently and they aren't open to believing a God of compassion and love cares about them. Whatever the reason, I can almost guarantee that if I pray before I go, if I pray on my way, if I pray for their hearts to be softened... they aren't going to throw me out. They will welcome a visit and open up a little.

You don't have to preach to them...you just must GO! God will pave the way for them to hear what is intended for them. And, if you've prayed about it, you will have the words to speak, or a zipper over your mouth to let them talk. Either way, GO!

8/1/21
TSW

Keep

The Webster dictionary describes "keep" as meaning - "to watch over or defend, to take care of."

It is mentioned 5 times in Psalm 121 ESV. *"He will not let your foot be moved; He who keeps you will not slumber. (v.3) The Lord is your keeper; the Lord is your shade on your right hand. (v.5) The Lord will keep you from all evil; He will keep your life. (v.7) The Lord will keep your going out and your coming in from this time forth and forevermore. (v. 8)"*

What does it mean to you to keep something? It may be a trinket from long ago, it may be a letter from a loved one that is gone, or even an heirloom piece...regardless, it is a special part of our life and history.

So, then, think about how God "keeps" us....

When our minds are whirling from devastating news... GOD KEEPS US.

When things seem frenzied and uncertain...GOD KEEPS US.

When we're lying in bed and can't fathom another day... GOD KEEPS US.

The maker of heaven and earth is keeping us close. He already knew that we would be going through whatever it is, so it is no surprise to Him. He will not slumber while we are hurting. Sometimes it may seem like He is sleeping on the job, but He is as close as the "shade of our hand" and is just waiting for us to reach out to Him.

10/17/21
TSW

A Good Soul Searching

"Put not your trust in princes, in a son of man, in whom there is no salvation. When his breath departs, he returns to the earth; on that very day his plans perish."
Psalm 146: 3-4 ESV

What are you putting your hope in? What is your focus on? Do your life plans include Jesus?

Don't get me wrong, there are needs...then there are NEEDS. Like I NEED "always discreet" or else I'd be doing laundry quite often. I NEED my medication, that keeps me on track. We all need the basics. Food, water, and a roof over our head! But are we so focused on what we can fill our house with, what we can fill our closets with, that we forget that the stuff we're so driven to find, will stay right here on this earth when we return to dust? Are we going to the grocery store or Amazon and filling our carts with things that aren't on the list, just to fill a void in our "self"?

What we need is a soul, heart, body and mind searching for all that God wants us to be. Not what we want for ourselves. What we need is to ask ourselves when we are searching for the next best thing? Are we spending quality time as a family? Are we listening or praying for

God to show us what we truly need? Are we showing others who God is or rushing through our day without even a glance at those around us?

Who or what are you putting your hope in? If you were gone today, think about what your legacy would be... would people see the things you collected or the God of your heart?

10/20/21
TSW

The Good Stuff

The other day I was sitting in the car wash and as it sprayed the pretty colorful soap onto the windows it began to coat the car with the good stuff that would help get it clean.

Isn't that how it is when we spend daily time with God? He coats our hearts and minds with "the good stuff" leaving us feeling clean and refreshed.

That is why it is so very important to spend quality uninterrupted time with God. It may have to be in your car on your way to work, or sitting at a sporting event, or holding up in the bathroom a little longer just to get some quiet time...but do it! Without this time, you are leaving your heart and mind open to the lies and plots of the enemy! He will do whatever it takes to make us feel like what we have isn't enough! Or find the opening to our weakness and make it fester until we give in to his lies.

Psalm 46 depicts a story of the mountains giving way... total chaos in our lives, a health crisis, schedule changes without warning, someone attacking us on social media and the list goes on... nevertheless, God is our refuge in present times! He can be our strength if we'd only "pick it up"! He wants to be within us, guiding us, holding us, lifting us.

One of the most famous verses in the bible is *Psalm 46:10 NIV*...instead of giving in to the lies of the enemy today, *"BE STILL, know that HE IS GOD"* and He'll "cover your life with the good stuff".

11/13/2021
TSW

JOY

The word "Joy" is the advent focus for this week.

As I awoke this morning the song "Joy unspeakable" came to my mind. Then I started to think of all the songs I know that have "joy" in them and they flooded my mind.

As I opened my first devotional book the very first thought was "No one can take away the joy and blessings that Christ gives us. We can find joy in Christ even when we are in pain. Joy cannot be erased by sorrow, loss, disappointment, or failure. It is a happiness that sees a rainbow through tears."

Then I opened my book "Do Something Beautiful for God", the essential teachings of Mother Teresa. The last sentence spoke to me. "The joy with which you look at your home ~ all this is God's love in the world today."

I have found it hard this year to find Christmas 'joy'. Several things with mom have been happening and my body has been hurting more than ever. I've had more bad days than good it seems, and it takes strength that I know only comes from God to get through. But today, I'm choosing to see the love...the JOY... that God gives

SO freely. It is my responsibility to pick it up. When I do, I know I will not be disappointed!

So today, every time you hear the word "JOY" grab onto it and let His joy flood your whole being.

12/13/21
TSW

Psalm 23

Yesterday I woke with the 23rd Psalm on my mind. Maybe the Lord knew I was anxious about my day which consisted of driving to an appointment two hours away. Morning traffic, bathroom opportunities, waiting in the car for John, (Since Covid was rampant and we could not go in with our loved one). I kept coming back to one part of the prayer where it says, *"Even though I walk through the valley of the shadow." Psalm 23:4 ESV*

Have you ever felt that you had a cloud hanging over your head? I'm not just talking about the Ohio normal! Some days you just don't feel in your right mindset to deal with the day ahead. Your anxious thoughts start running as soon as you open your eyes and your feet hit the floor.

Read further in verse 4. What comes after *"I will fear no evil, for You are with me." (ESV)* God is saying to us that NO MATTER WHAT clouds or shadows are hanging around, He will be with us. So, all our anxious, sometimes numbing thoughts are for nothing but letting the enemy win.

Guess what? There was no traffic, there were rest areas spaced perfectly and John's appointment did not take that long. When we arrived home, I was relaxing, scrolling through Facebook and in my memories was this thought. "When you're going through the valley of the shadow, just turn your back to the shadow and look to the light."

To have a shadow, there must be a light source. So instead of focusing on the shadows, turn into the One True Light and face your day!

1/6/2022
TSW

Love His Way

The New American Standard Version mentions the word "love" 541 times. Yet Jesus himself only mentions it 3 times in the whole Bible.

All three are in *John 13:34-36 NASV "A new command I give you: Love one another. As I have loved you, so that you may love one another. By this all men will know that you are my disciples, if you love one another."*

Isn't it so expected? After all God is love right? To know God, we should show love...His love.

It's SO very hard sometimes, and many times I must go back...and back....and back to change my attitudes toward others. I just want to scream to God, "REALLY? I'm suffering here too, yet I'm supposed to reach out, make time, go the extra mile to show love?!" What about me? Isn't that His whole point?

Jesus himself suffered to the point of death. FOR US! The least we can do is bake a cake, go visit or simply pick up the phone to check on someone. Okay God, I get it! It still isn't easy sometimes.

Today being Valentine's Day, why not start showing love now. Make a new plan that every time you feel down, are in pain, or are overwhelmed instead of screaming out, reach out to others. Others that are alone, going through a rough patch, or just someone who you haven't talked to in a while. Each and every time you do, all of your troubles or pain will diminish. Believe me, I know. I live it.

2-14-2022
TSW

Curveball

Chances are you already know that life can throw curve balls in EVERY area of your life all at once. We've all experienced it. We've all screamed "Really God? What else?"

These last three weeks, for me, have been beyond a curveball! I'm telling you that MANY times I have hit bottom. My crisis started off with Evan having a terrible night of sleep and I then had no sleep going into all of it.

Flooded basement means most of the stuff goes into a dumpster or the garage. Means getting pictures and estimates for replacements. Means DAYS of people in and out of your house to clean, tear out drywall and dry out. ETC... But it was revealed that we have 4 major leaks in the exterior walls which will now be fixed although beyond expensive and messy inside and out. (BLESSING-no future mold issues)

Testing on my left lower leg (which has been bad for years but over the last 4 months has worsened) due to times of nauseating, debilitating pain. (BLESSING- up until now, I have not had a foot doctor...he is new at my orthopedic doctor's office, and I love his bedside manner!)

Mom went through yet another severe UTI the week of the flood, so she did not tell me how bad it was. I found out that it was BAD. Vomiting, headaches and a fever. (BLESSING - they got her on the right med, and she didn't end up in the hospital)

Dylan & Sam lost a baby. Our grandchild. She continues to have cramping, labor like pains. She and Dylan are struggling terribly with this loss. Grandma & Grandpa as well. (BLESSING- TBD)

Remember that this is all happening in the middle of a bridal shower this weekend, which I am planning and the upcoming wedding in May.

I do not tell you any of this to get sympathy because again, I know we've all been there. I tell you this because I am choosing to see a blessing. Yes, I fall apart, but God in His mercy picks me up and holds me together. Seeing the good in all situations is a choice.

Sometimes we get so stuck in the "Mire" of situations that we complain and start to expect negative outcomes then it's a vicious cycle to get out of it. How hard it is for those around us to see Jesus in us, if we are complaining and stuck in the pit?

Act 1:8 TLB says "But when the Holy Spirit has come upon you, you will receive power to testify about me with great effect, to the people in Jerusalem, throughout Judea, in

Samaria, and to the ends of the earth, about my death and resurrection."

I want you to know, you CAN crawl out of anything if you reach for God's hand.

He's waiting.

3/15/2022
TSW

Not Forgotten

Have you ever felt forgotten? It happens to the best of us. In good and bad times. We wonder, is there anyone out there that even cares what we are going through?

Today in my two separate devotionals, one written in 2020 and the other written in 2018, both mention the word "forgotten". One phrase says, "In hard times we must remember, if we have received Christ, He cannot forget us, and we cannot forget Him." In the other it says, "The Lord's hand is not too short to provide for you, and He has not forgotten you, but He wants you to trust Him in the hard time."

Isn't it an amazing promise that even when we are at our lowest, when we forget who has gotten us to where we are today...God does not forget us.

Share that truth with others so that He gets all the Glory and others may be impressed with His love.

"God is not unjust; he will not forget your work and the love you have shown Him as you have helped His people and continue to help them. We want each of you to show this same diligence to the very end, so that what you hope for

may be fully realized. We do not want you to become lazy, but to imitate those who through faith and patience inherit what has been promised." Hebrews 6:10-12 NIV

4/14/22
TSW

Control

"This is the confidence we have in approaching God: that if we ask anything according to His will, He hears us. And if we know that He hears us—whatever we ask—we know that we have what we asked of Him." 1 John 5:14-15 NIV

WOW.... How many times do we pray- plead - ask of God - throw it all at His capable feet and then let it go? Walk away? It clearly states here that if we ask according to His will, He hears us! That we should know that we will have what we have asked of Him! "Will have", doesn't mean today. It means that we can trust Him that *"He works all things for our good" Romans 8:28 NIV*. That *"He is faithful" 1 Thessalonians 5:24 NIV*. So why is it SO hard to walk away after we pray for something or someone? Simple... Control.

We as humans always like a little control over our lives. Our lack of faith in God, results in doubt, and the enemy loves anything that takes our eyes off God. He will weasel his way into that crack and soon it's a canyon and we have trouble finding our way back.

2 Corinthians 4: 16-18 NIV says: "Therefore we do not lose heart. Though outwardly we are wasting away, yet inwardly we are being renewed day by day. For our light and momentary troubles are achieving for us an eternal glory that far outweighs them all. So, we fix our eyes not on what is seen, but on what is unseen, since what is seen is temporary, but what is unseen is eternal." Keeping our eyes on Jesus defeats the enemy! He has no choice but to leave and go find some other cracks to break open! He is working out everything that concerns you! Do not let the need for control in your life disrupt God's best for your life.

5/2/22
TSW

The Simple Answer

50 years ago today, my mom gave birth to me...I nearly killed her after delivering me at 10 pounds, but that's another story!

Yesterday I had an interview call with the surgery nurse for my upcoming 3rd ankle/leg surgery on May 24th. She confirmed my birthday and said wow, happy early birthday! I said, yes, it's the big 5-0! After that, we started going through my medical history and past procedure list. I said to her after going over it; you must think, "wow, how'd you ever get to be 50!?"

My answer is simple. God. I am not quite sure how people who do not have a close relationship with God do it...get through life. It's a chaotic world we live in and without it I would be on my back, struggling to make it through a day. Stuck in the pit of despair. Lately the image of a hand coming up out of the water reaching toward heaven with a hand reaching down to grab it has been flashing in my mind. It reminds me of the bible verse below.

Psalm 40:2-5 NLT "He lifted me out of the pit of despair, out of the mud and the mire. He set my feet on solid ground and steadied me as I walked along. He has given me a new song to sing, a hymn of praise to our God. Many will see what he has done and be amazed. They will put their trust in the Lord. Oh, the joys of those who trust the Lord, who have no confidence in the proud or in those who worship idols. O Lord my God, you have performed many wonders for us. Your plans for us are too numerous to list. You have no equal. If I tried to recite all your wonderful deeds, I would never come to the end of them."

How do you get through the day? Are you relying on your own futile strength? Are you starting the day with a prayer of thanks and protection against the enemy's attacks? Are you praying for His will for your day? If you aren't, you are missing out on the "new song and joy" that only He can give. Not everything will be perfect, but everything that comes your way will seem like small beans instead of majestic mountains!

I challenge you to try it and reap the benefits that serving an amazing God can have.

5/18/22
TSW

Where Would We Be?

We've all thought about it. We've all asked the question what if. What would life be like, if?

There was a time in my life when I was unfaithful to John, we sat on the couch talking about visitation schedules and who was going to pay what and where I would go. It was a hard talk. Especially since we were only about 5 years in! The kids were little! I tell you this because at that time I never pictured the life I have now. I was so far away from God that I couldn't see my way back. The scary thing is, I did not have a care in the world! The devil had wrapped his slimy hands around me, and he wasn't letting go.

During this conversation I needed a smoke and went onto the back porch and surveyed the landscape. At that moment I had an overwhelming need to scream..." HELP ME GOD!" At the top of my lungs, I did. Unless you've experienced it you cannot understand. God wrapped me up and the enemy scattered. The chains that enbondaged my heart were gone!

I went back into the house where John was and told him how very sorry I was and that I wanted to make it work. Thank You Heavenly Father for Your mercy! It was a long road but here we are going to celebrate 30 years in September. There is no place I'd rather be than beside him.

Ezekiel, 36: 24-26 NIV says, "For I will take you out of the nations; I will gather you from all the countries and bring you back into your own land. I will sprinkle clean water on you, and you will be clean; I will cleanse you of all your impurities and of all your idols. I will give you a new heart and put a new spirit in you; I will remove from you your heart of stone and give you a heart of flesh. And I will put my Spirit in you and move you to follow my decrees and be careful to keep my laws."

That day, that is what God did for me! He restored my hardened blinded heart and gave me my life. My life with my husband, kids and extended family.

Do you have a story like this? Have you ever been so far away from God, you didn't recognize yourself? Maybe you have a story of something in your life where the enemy had a grip. Share it with others so they know what God can do!

All three of my devotional books this morning are about breaking the cycle of bondage and sin. If you find yourself in this situation, please reach out personally and I will pray. I will pray that you can hand over your will and selfish desires to live your best life. A life with eternal promises of hope. Shout out to God and hand it all over to say "Yes" to everything God has to offer.

"It is wonderful what miracles God works in wills that are utterly surrendered to Him"

Hannah Whitall Smith.

6/13/22
TSW

Prepared

"Always be prepared to give an answer to everyone who asks you to give the reason for the hope that you have. But do this with gentleness and respect, keeping a clear conscience, so that those who speak maliciously against your good behavior in Christ may be ashamed of their slander."
1 Peter 3:15-16 NIV

I believe it's always been part of my DNA to be prepared. I think ahead of every step I take. Most times I think ahead of everybody else's step too. It's just my nature. Things like, making sure there are tissues in the glove box just in case. Making sure my grocery list is in order before I go to the store. Making sure I have all the necessities sitting right beside me before I sit down after a long day.

Let's think of the word "prepared" in a different manner. What about the times you run into someone you haven't seen for a long time, and you start talking about life? Do you happen to mention the struggles you've been going through and Who helped you get through them? Are we uncomfortable talking about Jesus and the hope we find in Him and just glaze over "life" and act like everything's peachy?

Peter is telling a crowd to be prepared to give an answer for their hope. This means, even those that get on our bad side and under our skin! I think maybe even more so with those folks, because they need to see Jesus in us regardless of how we feel about them. Isn't that the whole point to what Peter is saying? When I think about Jesus I think about a calm, gentle presence. Maybe we might be the only connection they have to that kind of life.

Maybe you're not a person that prepares for things, you don't really have to be.

It's simple, when you are out and about running errands, at social events, and you run into someone, all you need to say in your mind and heart are "Lord give me the words to be Jesus to this person." That's all the preparedness you need.

10/1/22
TSW

More Time

I bet many of us would agree that time is an eluding commodity. It comes and goes so fast that you wonder where the day went. When I think of time I think of many things, not just my calendar and the surmounting things that seem to come up, that will end up occupying more time than I want(ed) to give. We've all been there!

I think of my dad, my grandma and mostly my brother who was only 46 when he died. Loved ones or people that we know that have died, do you think they thought they had more time? I look at the way it all happened with my brother. That day he had been having shoulder pain and ignored it, thinking it was from the work he had been doing on the remodel. If he would have gone to the hospital instead of work...would he still be here? Only God knows that answer. And only God knows that answer for you or me. Our responsibility is to take care of what God has given us... His vessel.

But in losing someone, I also think of whether they have more time to get their heart and life right with God. We all want everyone to get their lives together and get into a serious relationship with Jesus.

"But you must not forget this one thing, dear friends: A Day is like a thousand years to the Lord, and a thousand

years is like a day. The Lord isn't really being slow about His promise, as some people think. No, He is being patient for your sake. He does not want anyone to be destroyed but wants everyone to repent."
2 Peter 3:8-9 NIV

Isn't it beyond amazing? God is patiently waiting on us to get our acts together. He wants us all to succeed and make it to the ultimate destination that He has been preparing for us.

I pray this New Year 2023 you're not just making frivolous resolutions just to say you did and a month later stop. This year, why not make a serious relationship with God the priority. My last devotional this year by Charles Stanley says this: "There is a new year ahead of you, and God wants to work through you and demonstrate His power and wisdom in your life as you live out His purposes."

My grandma had a note on her fridge that stuck with me even after she was gone.

"Do it Now". She made that note after not calling a loved one and then finding out they had passed. We could apply this insight to MANY areas of our lives.

12/31/22
TSW

Joy?

*"Consider it pure joy, my brothers and sisters,
whenever you face trials of many kinds"*
James 1:2 NIV

For Our Good?

*"And we know that in all things God works
for the good of those who love him, who have
been called according to his purpose."*
Romans 8:28 NIV

How?.Why?....

We've all been there. The questions of our hearts and minds during unparalleled circumstances. How are we supposed to adapt? Why is God allowing this trial?

Those questions are a human response to tragic times in our lives. But God wants us to be more like Him. To be more like Him, He asks us to "Count it all joy when we experience trials. To see that "All things work together for our good." Are You kidding God?! Some days you wanna throw in the towel, stay in bed, pull the covers over your head and scream!

Two times in my life I have had a sudden loss. This was exactly how I felt at first. I withdrew and thoughts swirled through my head. The "How's and Why's" were at the forefront of my mind. But then came the promises of our loving Heavenly Father.

"Don't be afraid, for I am with you. Don't be discouraged, for I am your God. I will strengthen you and help you. I will hold you up with my victorious right hand." Isaiah 41:10 NLT

"This is my command, be strong and courageous! Do not be afraid or discouraged. For the Lord your God is with you wherever you go." Joshua 1:9 NLT

And then the human side of me began to die and the heart of Jesus came through and I remembered... PRAYER.

"Don't worry about anything, but in everything, through prayer and petition with thanksgiving, present your requests to God. And the peace of God that surpasses all understanding, will guard your hearts and minds in Christ Jesus." Philippians 4:6-7 CSB

"For I can do everything THROUGH CHRIST who gives me strength." Philippians 4:13 NLT

If we curled up in a ball and withdrew during trials, we would not be fulfilling the call of Christ. We can have a moment to mourn the loss, whether it be life, a job, our health, a friendship...the list goes on... BUT we are to be witnesses to those around us that God calls us to serve and give our testimony. Is it hard? Absolutely! But thankfully we have a great big God walking beside us, pulling us up out of the miry clay, placing our feet on the solid rock.

4/18/2023
TSW

Laid Out

There's an old song rolling around in my head this morning. The word "prostrate" is in it but I just can't bring the song up in my mind. So, I looked up the definition, this is what it means; "lying stretched out on the ground with one's face downward." The second way it can be used; "of distress, exhaustion, or illness, reduce to extreme physical weakness."

Now, I don't know about you, but these days I do not get on the floor very often! If I do, I can barely get up and my back gets out of whack and my body hurts. So, the thought of lying face down on the floor is not very appealing. However, isn't that what God asks us to do when presenting our needs to Him? To earnestly seek Him? To lay down.

Hebrews 11:6 NLT says, "And it is impossible to please God without faith. Anyone who wants to come to Him must believe that God exists and that He rewards those who sincerely seek Him."

Notice in the second definition the words exhaustion, reduced to extreme physical weakness. How many times is our body so weary we just don't think we can go another minute? I know for me this is a daily occurrence. And if someone asked me how I get things done my answer is always the same "God's strength."

In our prayers, we are limiting God by not laying it all out. He already knows our inner thoughts. Our weaknesses. But so does Satan. And when we are not exposing ourselves, seeking God earnestly and believing that He is able, we give Satan the crack he needs to get into our thoughts.

So, this morning when you petition God with your prayers, you don't have to be on the floor to earnestly seek Him, but you do need to be "prostrated" before Him with your mind and your heart. Completely laid out!

6/18/23
TSW

Sustenance

Are you relying on God as much as you rely on social media? As much as you rely on Amazon? As much as you rely on a paycheck? As much as you rely on your calendar?

Yesterday the word sustenance came up in the sermon I listened to by Charles Stanley. He said, "the attitude behind prayer must come from a life of obedience that is looking to God for sustenance for everything."

We think of sustenance as nutritional. But it is so much more than that! It is the strength to get through a day. It is the peace that passes all understanding when your day is chaotic. It is the Hope that we look for when you don't see a way.

When you look up another word for sustenance it comes up with "daily bread". Even in the Lord's prayer that is mentioned. Daily bread is not only nutritional it is the word of God. We need it daily. Sometimes a moment by moment. Without it we will not be able to weather life.

In *John 6:48 NIV, Jesus says, "I Am the Bread of Life".* He's not talking about food. He's talking about His sustaining presence in our lives when we look to Him for all things! He's talking about the way that we can live a Holy life through Him and have eternal life forever in Heaven.

In my current devotional book this is a quote from this morning.

"Thoughts of independent righteousness are a grand illusion.... so, there is no reason to boast. There's nothing for which we can take credit. All praise, honor, worship and service go to God and God alone. He saw us. He sustains us. He matures us. He protects us." Paul Tripp

Without Him we are just an empty vessel that will wander through life without direction, without peace, without strength and ultimately without heaven.

9/24/23
TSW

Reign in My Brain

Do you, like me, wakeup and your brain is running a mile a minute with 27 tabs open? Or you look around and see all the tasks ahead for the day?

When we sit before the Lord, we must purposefully ask God to reign in our brains! Someone once suggested sitting with a sticky note so that if your mind wanders you got something down then leave it there so you can continue with God, free of distractions. Another tip is to leave your phone elsewhere or face down, so you're not tempted to pick it up.

In the Old Testament there are 2 verses to look up. Each mentions the word "seek". Seek means: to search for; to request; to aim or try. Meaning, when we are searching, seeking out time with God, He will help close the tabs so we can solely focus on Him.

Deuteronomy 4:29 NIV tells us about the Israelites and how they will worship man-made gods and get comfortable in their daily lives. But- *"if they will seek God with all their hearts and souls, they will find Him."* How many times do we do that ourselves? We get comfortable just sailing along having a haphazard meditation time with God. Doing things that don't mean diddly squat to God's

Kingdom? God is knowable and wants to be known. But we must want to know Him better!

God is all knowing - "He searches our hearts."

1 Chronicles 28:9 NLT "For the Lord sees every heart and knows every plan and thought" But David first tells his son Solomon that he must "learn to know the God of your ancestors intimately. Worship and serve him with your whole heart and a willing mind." He goes on to say "if you seek Him, you will find him. But if you forsake Him, He will reject you forever."

Can you imagine being rejected by God? One vision that comes to mind is at heaven's gates! I surely don't want God to turn His face from me and say, *"depart from me."* *Matthew 25:41 NIV*

11/28/23
TSW

Faith-Full-ness

"Because of the LORD's great love, we are not consumed, for His compassions never fail. They are new every morning; great is Your faithfulness. I say to myself, "The LORD is my portion; therefore, I will wait for Him." Lamentations 3:22-24 NIV

The Life Application Bible's description of these verses reminds us that God's mercies are new every morning. His faithfulness will endure! Are you leaning into your faith, or are you relying on yourself? Others? What the world is offering for solutions to your "suffering?"

Romans 5:3-5 NIV says that we are to "glory" in our suffering, so many days I am not shouting glory! I am overwhelmed by pain. Pain shooting when I walk and pain when I sit. It goes on to say that it leads to perseverance, character and hope. Paul explains that we will "become" but until then we must "overcome" (Life Application Bible)

Through each trial we endure, whether pain, work, relationships, finances - the list can go on and on. It is not always for us to fix or engineer a solution. Most often God has a lesson involved and wants us to grow and discover what He wants for our lives. He wants to see if we are "full of faith" or waiting on Him, glorifying Him in the pause.

"...though now, for a little while you may have to suffer grief in all kinds of trials. These have come so that the proven genuineness of your faith- of greater worth than gold, which perishes even though refined by fire." 1 Peter 1:6-7 NIV. Peter is telling them that it's a refining process. It's taking away all our impurities through the fires of life. Offering us something that cannot perish!

If we are walking around grumbling and complaining every time the apple basket is knocked over, or when we are suffering in any way, how is that glorifying God? The old saying "WWJD" - it's true! We need others to see Jesus in our reactions to the trials. *Romans 14:13 NIV, "make up your minds to not put any stumbling blocks or obstacles in front of your brother or sister."* How we react under pressure is key to leading others to know our great big God.

I pray that others see Jesus' light through us!

11/30/23
TSW

Lifted and Able

Many moons ago due to my selfishness and sin, John and I were at the point of separating. We were sitting on the couch talking about the visit schedule for the kids. I remember it just like it was yesterday, I was held in Satan's clutches. He had convinced me that life was greener with the things of the world. After many tears, thoughts were swirling around (Isn't that just like the enemy? He wants us to be in turmoil all balled up in knots. He is the master of confusion and doubt.)

Anywho, I needed a break - so I went out to the back porch, I smoked back then (another clutch of Satan) and as I'm standing there, I remember it so vividly, I literally looked up to heaven and screamed "GOD HELP ME!!!"

I don't know if you've ever felt like things were so far out of whack, like you didn't even know who you were anymore - but that is exactly where I was at that time. I'm serious when I say, at that time it was just as David wrote in *Psalms 40:1-3 NLT* "*He heard my cry, He lifted me out of the slimy pit of despair, out of the mud and the mire, He set my feet on solid ground and steadied me as I walked along. He has given me a new song to sing, a hymn of praise to our God. Many will see and fear the Lord and put their trust in Him.*"

HE LIFTED ME OUT! It was life-altering! I went in and told John that this was not what I wanted, and we began a long hard road to healing.

God is so good! Even just writing about it puts me in awe of Him, giving me so much thankfulness to God in heaven.

I don't know what has you in Satan's clutches. I don't know where you are on your faith journey - but God is able!

Are you in a fiery furnace like Shadrach, Meshach and Abednego? God is able to save you!

"If we are thrown into the blazing furnace, the God we serve is able to deliver us from it, and he will deliver us from Your Majesty's hand." Daniel 3:17 NIV

Are you suffering, tempted by the evil of worldly pleasures? Jesus is able to help you because He himself was tempted.

"Because he himself suffered when he was tempted, he is able to help those who are being tempted." Hebrews 2:18 NIV

Whatever road you're going down, *"He is able to save completely those who come to God - through Him, because He always lives to intercede for them." Hebrews 7:25 NIV*

"Now to Him who is able to do immeasurably more than all we ask or imagine, according to His power that is at work within us, to Him be the glory in the church and in Christ Jesus throughout all generations, forever and ever! Amen."
Ephesians 3:20-21 NIV

12/2/23
TSW

"Feed My Sheep"

"When they had finished eating, Jesus said to Simon Peter, "Simon son of John, do you love me more than these?" "Yes, Lord," he said, "you know that I love you." Jesus said, "Feed my lambs." Again, Jesus said, "Simon son of John, do you love me?" He answered, "Yes, Lord, you know that I love you."

Jesus said, "Take care of my sheep." The third time he said to him, "Simon son of John, do you love me?" Peter was hurt because Jesus asked him the third time, "Do you love me?" He said, "Lord, you know all things; you know that I love you." Jesus said, "Feed my sheep."

John 21:15-17 NIV

Do you ever wake up in the morning and ask Jesus "What can I do for you today, Lord?"

Oftentimes we have a full calendar, and you wonder how on earth are you going to be able to keep up, let alone have undistracted time with Jesus!

In John 21:15-17 NIV Jesus asks Simon Peter "Do you love Me?" Three times he said, "You know that I love you." How many times does a person have to be asked something before you believe their answer? Jesus was asking Simon Peter... "Do you love me more than these?" In today's world, maybe "these" are money, food, even your own family. Or maybe, it's a bad habit of shopping, drinking, smoking, overeating. Then there's just plain old busy-ness and overscheduling. Do we love Jesus more than all of it?

If all those things just mentioned are keeping you from loving Jesus completely, wholeheartedly, genuinely, for the sake of eternity... It's time to reevaluate! Jesus will not settle for second best and superficial answers. He knows all and He will get to the heart of the matter.

Do you love Jesus "more than these" Feed His sheep. That means we tell others who Jesus is, who he can be for them.

One of my childhood memory verses from quizzing is in Acts.

Jesus is telling His disciples that they "will receive power when the Holy Spirit comes on you, and you will be My witnesses in Jerusalem, in all Judea and Samaria, and to the ends of the earth." Acts 1:8 NIV

When we live life with the heart of Jesus we have the Holy Spirit, who gives us the ability to live with courage, boldness, insight, and authority of Jesus Christ. We need all these characteristics to Feed His lost sheep and point others to the One True God.

12/3/23
TSW

It Takes a Village

Do you like to do things "your way"? Have you ever sought the advice of others letting it go in one ear and out the other? Human nature does not like to hear honest truths. They sting a bit. But if the council is given in love, it should never put a wedge or sore spot within the relationship.

In the Bible, Solomon is known as the world's smartest man and when he is given, seeks and hears wise counsel, he prays and seeks discernment.

You've heard the old saying "it takes a village"? We need others! We are all on a different step of the journey to eternity.

"For a lack of guidance, a nation falls, but victory is through many advisers."
Proverbs 11:14 NIV

Isn't victory better than struggling to make sense of whatever you are facing? Yet, we let our pride get in the way. We let the enemy twist the advice and muddy it up a bit, just so that we can keep going and get our own way. We close our hearts and minds to truly hearing it.

"Plans fail for the lack of counsel but with many advisors they succeed" Proverbs 15:22 NIV

We have tunnel vision, one way thinking. When we ask for wisdom and discernment after receiving Godly counsel, it will require action at some point. It doesn't mean we run with it. It means we "hear it" then pray for God's Will. God will be faithful to show you, His way. He will give you the strength it takes to keep taking steps in the direction He has for your life.

But you have to be willing to "do the work". Sometimes its deep soul searching and purging!

Solomon had the chance to have anything he wanted in the world, yet he asked God for wisdom. (1 Kings 3:5-9 NIV) He didn't ask God to fix the problem, he asked for discernment to be a leader of the people.

If we surround ourselves with believers and Godly friends, we can know that God will use them at some point, to advise us along our journey. But we must be open to hear the hard stuff.

Having wisdom is a result of knowing and trusting God. Knowing God will lead to understanding and then we are able to share insight with others - therefore being a vital part of the village.

12/6/2023
TSW

Alone

"After He dismissed the crowd, He went up on a mountainside by Himself to pray. Later that night He was there alone."
Matthew 14:23 LAB

Each and every day I get up and have my quiet time with Jesus. Everything in the house is totally quiet. It's so peaceful. But recently I had to have major back surgery and I knew that at the hospital being on pain meds and the effects of surgery I'd be lacking in my ability to do so. Also the fact is, when I spend time with Jesus I have my Bible, a notebook, pens, highlighters, my phone for a podcast or quick scripture reference and of course my coffee, I couldn't see carrying all that to the hospital. Still while there I used my phone to read an emailed devotional and spend time alone with Jesus. It wasn't as convenient or quiet, but a necessary part of who I am in Christ.

You see, in the Bible, Jesus took time repeatedly to be alone with His Heavenly Father. He knew that witnessing, healing, preaching, keeping the disciples in line and traveling would've taken a toll on His body if He did not have times of refreshing. Times of praying and listening.

It's like that for us here on earth every day. We are pressed with the "to do" lists of the day, the workplace drama, doctor appointments, the responsibilities of a household, over committing to organizations or events, and the list could go on. That is why it is so very important to carve out an hour every day. An hour dedicated to digging into God's word, listening for His direction and "seeking Him." *Psalm 105:4 LAB, says, "Look to the Lord and seek His strength; seek His face always."*

You say, "but my day is so full already, how in the world can I get an hour alone?" I promise you, if you commit your day to God first, as soon as you open your eyes, and tell your Heavenly Father that you need the time alone for refreshing to get your eyes focused on God...He'll make a way, you just need to listen and do it.

2/13/2024
TSW

Weighted Down

Yesterday at church the pastor was discussing Holy Week. After the Passover had taken place and Jesus' ride through Jerusalem on the donkey, Jesus was telling the Greeks about why He must die. He knew that He would be crucified and why. The pastor then asked the question, "How do you think the weight of all the world's sin weighed on Him? Did it make Him anxious? Make Him weary?" Of course it did!

John 12:27-28 NIV says *"Now my soul is troubled, and what shall I say? Father, save me from this hour? No, it is for this very reason that I came to this hour. Father, glorify Your name!"*

Jesus knew. He knew that the death He would endure would be cruel and beyond painful, yet He praised and glorified His Father.

How many of us, would be or are truly praising Jesus when we suffer pain or tragedy? When our kids are suffering and there is nothing, we can do about it? When we are overwhelmed by employment? Relationships? Or lack of them?

It's hard for me to imagine that God sent His son to be born to walk alongside us on this earth and then let him die such a horrific death. All because I'm a selfish human, who messes up daily that needs saving from myself and an eternal death.

If you back up a couple verses in John 12:25 NIV, Jesus says, *"Anyone who loves their life will lose it, while anyone who hates their life in this world will keep it for eternal life."*

The Life Application Bible explains it like this: "We must be so committed to living for Jesus, that we hate our lives in comparison. This does not mean we are to live careless or destructive lives. Rather we are willing to die if doing so glorifies Christ. We must disown the dominating self-centeredness rule of the world and transfer control to Jesus." WOW!

Imagine how heavy the cross got as He made His way up the hill to Golgotha. Now imagine Him carrying not only the cross, but every sin of ours and the worlds, on top of that! He carried it for us! He took it onto His shoulders so that we could have the hope of eternal life with Him in Heaven someday.

Stop letting whatever weighs you down take control of your life. Give it to Jesus. He's always ready and willing to handle it.

3/18/2024
TSW

"56"

In my adult years, too many times to count, the number '56' would come up in some form. Change I received from an order, where the gas pump stopped, a license plate I just happened to look at. You get the picture. Well, somewhere along the lines, the enemy planted the thought that I was going to die at that age. (insert wide eyed emoji!) Yeah, it was kind of scary, considering now I am 51!

So, sometime within the last 3 years I decided I was going to fight back. I started to look up any book of the Bible that might have 56 chapters. Guess what? There are only two. Psalms and Isaiah. Psalms 56's theme according to the Life Application Bible is "Trusting God's care in the midst of fear. When all seems dark, one truth still shines bright. When God is for us, those against us will never succeed." What a great truth!

Psalm 56 NIV
"Be merciful to me, my God,
for my enemies are in hot pursuit;
all day long they press their attack.
My adversaries pursue me all day long;
in their pride many are attacking me.

When I am afraid, I put my trust in you.
In God, whose word I praise—
in God I trust and am not afraid.
What can mere mortals do to me?
All day long they twist my words;
all their schemes are for my ruin.
They conspire, they lurk,
they watch my steps,
hoping to take my life.

Because of their wickedness
do not let them escape;
in your anger, God, bring the nations down.
Record my misery;
list my tears on your scroll—
are they not in your record?
Then my enemies will turn back
when I call for help.
By this I will know that God is for me.
In God, whose word I praise,
in the Lord, whose word I praise—
in God I trust and am not afraid.
What can man do to me?
I am under vows to you, my God;
I will present my thank offerings to you.
For you have delivered me from death
and my feet from stumbling,
that I may walk before God
in the light of life."

Today and from now on, whenever the enemy throws out the olé '56', I'm going to throw this chapter right back at him!

James 4:7 NIV says, "Submit yourselves, then, to God. Resist the devil, and he will flee from you.

What is something getting thrown into your face on a daily, weekly, monthly basis? Choose to throw it back at the enemy! If it's not for your good, it's not from God. Because *"And we know that in all things God works for the good of those who love him" Romans 8:28 NIV*

3/26/2024
TSW

Happily, Blessed

Every day when I make coffee, I grab a Splenda-Stevia packet from the cupboard. On each packet they have a positive thought or quote. Kind of neat! Today it said, "Make time for what makes you happy." Now, I don't have a problem with being happy, in fact, my husband once called me "annoyingly optimistic". LOL. But how many times do we do things that make us happy and then we back pedal after doing whatever it was? Maybe it was "shopping till you drop" and then you look at your bank account and have buyers' remorse. Maybe it was taking a vacation to "get away" and then you need a vacation to recover.

If you open your Bible and look up the words happy and joy, you will find the same scripture passage. Matthew 5:3-12 NIV. Otherwise known as "The Beatitudes"

> *"Blessed are the poor in spirit,*
> *for theirs is the kingdom of heaven.*
> *Blessed are those who mourn,*
> *for they will be comforted.*
> *Blessed are the meek,*
> *for they will inherit the earth.*
> *Blessed are those who hunger and thirst for*
> *righteousness, for they will be filled.*

Blessed are the merciful,
for they will be shown mercy.
Blessed are the pure in heart,
for they will see God.
Blessed are the peacemakers,
for they will be called children of God.
Blessed are those who are persecuted
because of righteousness,
for theirs is the kingdom of heaven.
Blessed are you when people insult you, persecute
you and falsely say all kinds of evil against you
because of me. Rejoice and be glad, because great
is your reward in heaven, for in the same way they
persecuted the prophets who were before you."

Are you sure we have the right scripture? You see the words: "poor, hungry, and mourn!" That sure doesn't sound happy!

But being happy doesn't always mean things are peachy. It means that despite the hard things life brings, you can thrive and not merely survive. It means you look beyond to the Father in Heaven who gives you the "happy."

I'm sure you noticed that each verse starts with the word "blessed." The Life Application Bible summarizes the beatitudes like this: *"Being blessed means more than being happy. It describes the fortunate or privileged position of those that belong to Gods Kingdom. Being blessed by God means experiencing hope and joy, independent of outward circumstances."*

Are you truly happy? Truly blessed? Are you living with God in mind for all your planning? I'll be the first to admit that since I am a planner, sometimes I leave God in the dust. But I am learning that until I bring God right alongside me, I will have a rocky road that gets to be overwhelming. I'll have more times of unhappiness and disappointment that will get me down. When we keep God in the passenger seat and not the back seat, we can be truly happy and blessed.

"To open the door to such hope and joy, which leads to the deepest form or happiness, we must walk across the threshold of suffering, sacrifice and transformation."
(Life Application Bible summary continued)

4/9/2024
TSW

About the Author

Tami S. Wyatt is a wife, mother, and Mimi. Her passion has become to live boldly, sharing her faith, and telling others about God. Within her life story are countless examples of God's faithfulness and provision. At the early age of 12, she was paralyzed from the chest down, having to learn how to walk and write all over. Then at the age of 35 she was diagnosed with Multiple Sclerosis, then at age 39 Sjogrens Syndrome. Having to endure multiple surgeries she lives with chronic nerve and muscle pain as well as physical and social limitations.

She believes wholeheartedly in the mercy and grace that God gives daily and without the strength that He provides, she would not make it through each day.

"Three times I pleaded with the Lord to take it away from me. But He said to me, 'My grace is sufficient for you, My power is made perfect in weakness.' Therefore, I will boast all the more gladly about my weaknesses, so that Christ's power may rest on me. That is why, for Christ's sake I delight in weaknesses, in insults, and hardship, in persecutions, and difficulties. For when I am weak then I am strong."
2 Corinthians 12:8-10 NIV

"The Lord will fight for you, you only need be still."
Exodus 14:14 NIV

This was a very important verse when going through the sudden loss of her brother who was only 46 at the time.

"With man this is impossible, but with God, all things are possible." Matthew 19:26 NIV

A few years ago, in a devotional book she was reading, the author challenged the reader to get a blank 4x6 card and write the verse on it. This was to be a reminder that with God, all things are possible. She accepted the challenge and then started writing prayer requests, concerns, and joys on the card. It has grown to multiple layers of cards now, stapled together.

Printed in the United States
by Baker & Taylor Publisher Services